Syd Hoff's
DANNY AND THE DINOSAUR
A Very Dino Christmas

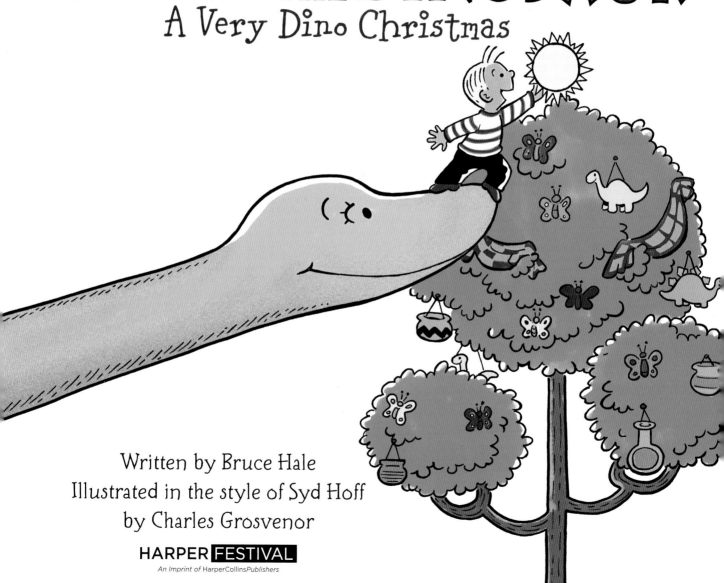

Written by Bruce Hale
Illustrated in the style of Syd Hoff
by Charles Grosvenor

HARPER FESTIVAL
An Imprint of HarperCollinsPublishers

HarperFestival is an imprint of HarperCollins Publishers.

Danny and the Dinosaur: A Very Dino Christmas
Copyright © 2017 by Anti-Defamation League Foundation, Inc.,
The Authors Guild Foundation, Inc., ORT America, Inc., United Negro College Fund, Inc.
For information address HarperCollins Children's Books, a division of HarperCollins Publishers,
195 Broadway, New York, NY 10007.
www.harpercollinschildrens.com

Library of Congress Control Number: 2016961851
ISBN 978-0-06-241046-7

Book design and typography by Jeff Shake
17 18 19 20 21 SCP 10 9 8 7 6 5 4 3 2 1
❖
First Edition

A little before Christmas, Danny invited his friend the dinosaur to visit him.

"Why is a tree growing inside your house?" asked the dinosaur. "And what's that funny-looking fruit?"

"Those are our Christmas tree and decorations," said Danny.

"And how about those socks over your fireplace?"
the dinosaur asked. "Are they drying out?"

"Those are Christmas stockings," said Danny. "It's a tradition.
Don't you have Christmas traditions?"

"Our traditions are more about eating and stomping," said the dinosaur. "I've never celebrated Christmas before." "Never?" said Danny.

"But I'd like to try." The dinosaur smiled. "Will you help?"

Danny and the dinosaur went back to the museum. "Hmm," said the dinosaur. "It doesn't look very Christmas-y, does it?" "Let's change that," said Danny.

They searched the exhibits until they found just the right tree.
Then they decorated it with many colorful things.

When they finished, the dinosaur looked at their work.
"It's missing something."
"Every Christmas tree needs a star," said Danny.

"Ooh!" said the dinosaur. "I know the perfect one."
And with Danny's help, he put it way up at the tippy top.

Danny and the dinosaur
found just the right stockings
to hang over the fireplace.

HARPER FESTIVAL
An Imprint of HarperCollins Publishers

Illustrations © 2017 by the Estate of Syd Hoff

Illustrations © 2017 by the Estate of Syd Hoff

Illustrations © 2017 by the Estate of Syd Hoff

Illustrations © 2017 by the Estate of Syd Hoff

Illustrations © 2017 by the Estate of Syd Hoff

Dear:

Have a Very
DINO
Christmas!

Love,

Dear:

Have a Very
DINO
Christmas!

Love,

Dear:

Have a Very
DINO
Christmas!

Love,

Dear:

Have a Very
DINO
Christmas!

Love,

Dear:

Have a Very
DINO
Christmas!

Love,

Dear:

Have a Very
DINO
Christmas!

Love,

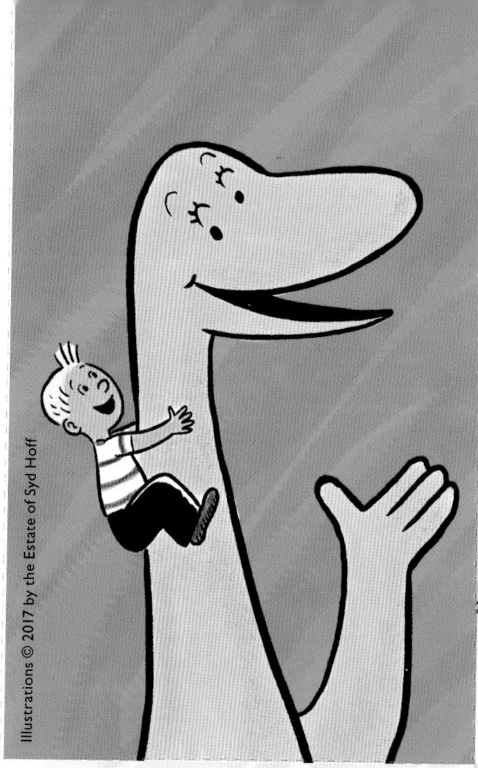

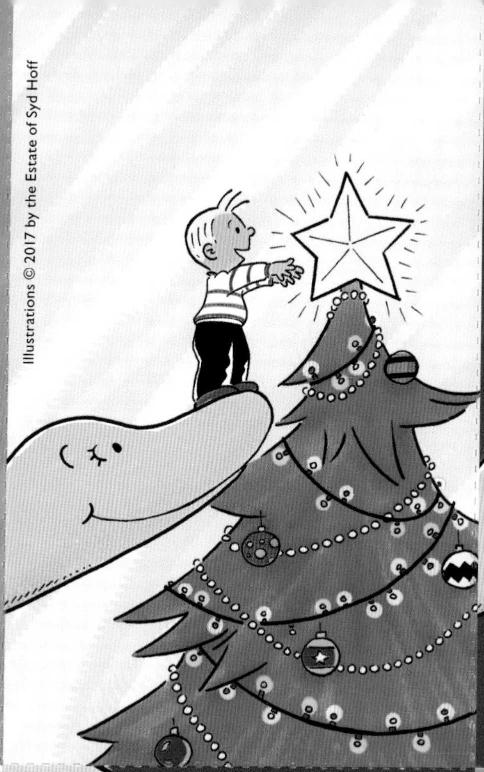

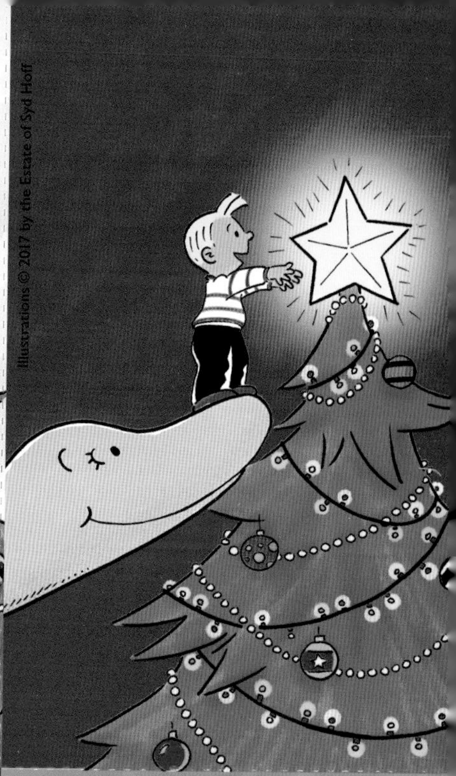

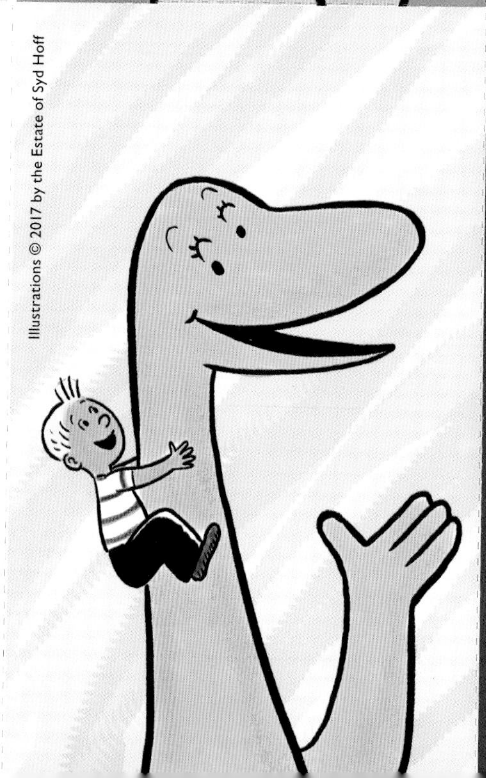

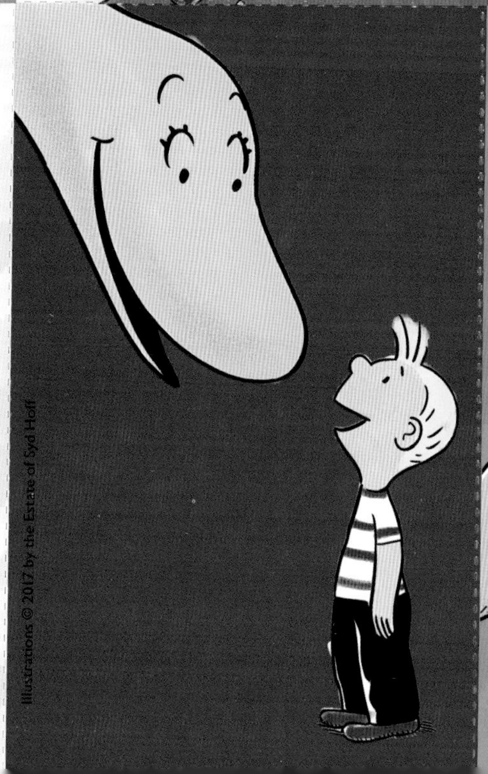

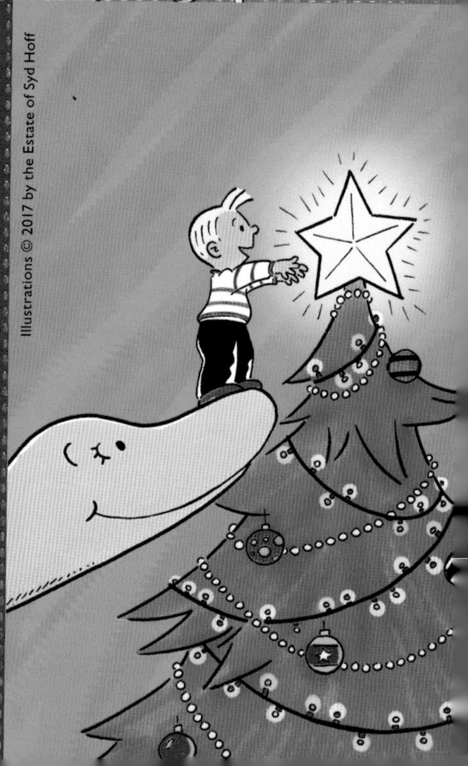

Dear:

Have a Very DINO Christmas!

Love,

Dear:

Have a Very DINO Christmas!

Love,

Dear:

Have a Very DINO Christmas!

Love,

Dear:

Have a Very DINO Christmas!

Love,

Dear:

Have a Very DINO Christmas!

Love,

Dear:

Have a Very DINO Christmas!

Love,

The museum was looking more
and more Christmas-y all the time.

Last of all, Danny and the dinosaur fancied up the great hall of the museum with just the right decorations.

"There. That should do it," said the dinosaur.
"Now this place looks like Christmas."

"What have you done?" shouted a bald man with glasses. He was the museum director. "You've made a mess of our museum. Bad dinosaur!"

Danny and the dinosaur hung their heads. All they wanted was to create some Christmas spirit.

But then a family approached. "We love your Christmas decorations," the woman told the museum director. "Very original."

"It's a Dino Christmas," said Danny.
"What a great idea!" said the man. "We're
telling everyone we know to come see it."

The family was true to their word. More and more people came to see how Danny and the dinosaur had decorated the museum. In fact, the museum had its busiest December ever.

"And it's all thanks to you," said the museum director to the dinosaur. "Would you please do us the honor of hanging the lights on our brand-new Christmas tree?"

So Danny and the dinosaur
strung up the twinkly lights
and turned them on.
Everyone went "Ooh!"

"Now we've got a new holiday tradition," said the museum director.
"And I want to wish everyone a Very Dino Christmas!"
"Hooray for Danny and the dinosaur!" the crowd cheered.
"Merry Christmas, everyone!" said Danny and the dinosaur.